Pebble® Plus

# Sand Tiger Sharks

A 4D Book

by Jody S. Rake

CAPSTONE PRESS
a capstone imprint

## Download the Capstone **4D** app!

- Ask an adult to download the Capstone 4D app.
- Scan the cover and stars inside the book for additional content.

When you scan a spread, you'll find fun extra stuff to go with this book! You can also find these things on the web at www.capstone4D.com using the password: sandtiger.01587

Pebble Plus is published by Capstone Press,
1710 Roe Crest Drive, North Mankato, Minnesota 56003
www.mycapstone.com

**Library of Congress Cataloging-in-Publication Data**
Names: Rake, Jody Sullivan, author.
Title: Sand tiger sharks : a 4D book / by Jody S. Rake.
Description: North Mankato, Minnesota : Capstone Press,
[2019] | Series: Pebble plus. All about sharks | Audience:
Age 4–7. | Includes bibliographical references and index.
Identifiers: LCCN 2018002872 (print) | LCCN 2018008476
(ebook) | ISBN 9781977101662 (eBook PDF) |
ISBN 9781977101587 (hardcover) | ISBN 9781977101624
(paperback)
Subjects: LCSH: Sand tiger shark—Juvenile literature.
Classification: LCC QL638.95.O3 (ebook) | LCC QL638.95.O3
R35 2019 (print) | DDC 597.3/4—dc23
LC record available at https://lccn.loc.gov/2018002872

**Editorial Credits**
Marissa Kirkman, editor; Charmaine Whitman, designer;
Kelly Garvin, media researcher; Kathy McColley, production
specialist

**Image Credits**
Getty Images/Gerard Soury, 21; Nature Picture Library/
Doug Perrine, 17; Newscom: Andy Murch/VWPics, 19,
Kelvin Aitken, 15, Michael Patrick O'Neill, 9; Shutterstock:
Barry Coleman, 13, Brent Bames, cover, Dray, 7, Maquiladora,
8, Rich Carey, 3, 24, sirtravelalot, 1, 5, Stefan Pircher, 11,
Willyam Bradbury, 23

## Note to Parents and Teachers

The All About Sharks set supports national curriculum standards for science related to the characteristics and behavior of animals. This book describes and illustrates sand tiger sharks. The images support early readers in understanding the text. The repetition of words and phrases helps early readers learn new words. This book also introduces early readers to subject-specific vocabulary words, which are defined in the Glossary section. Early readers may need assistance to read some words and to use the Table of Contents, Glossary, Read More, Internet Sites, Critical Thinking Questions, and Index sections of the book.

Printed and bound in China.
309

# Table of Contents

# Not as Scary as it Looks

A large shark floats above

the sandy ocean floor.

It is searching for food.

Snap! The sand tiger shark

grabs its meal.

A sand tiger shark's sharp, skinny teeth stick out. Its toothy mouth makes it look scary. But it is not a threat to humans.

# Slow Swimmers

Sand tiger sharks have bodies shaped like long, skinny footballs. Their dorsal fins are shaped like triangles. The top tail fin is much longer than the bottom one.

5 feet (1.5 meters)

7–10 feet (2 to 3 meters)

dorsal fins

Sand tiger sharks have brownish gray backs and white bellies. Most sand tiger sharks also have reddish brown spots on their backs. Their snouts are pointed and flat.

Sand tiger sharks live in warm waters close to shore. They are slow swimmers. If they stop swimming they sink to the bottom. These sharks swallow air to help them float.

## Hunting and Eating

Sand tiger sharks eat a lot of food.

They feed on many kinds of fishes.

They hunt on the ocean floor.

Special organs in their head

help them hunt for prey.

Sand tiger sharks hunt in groups.
They work together to herd fish.
This gives the whole group
plenty to eat.

17

## Sand Tiger Babies

Sand tiger pups hatch from eggs
inside their mother after nine months.
Two pups are born at a time.
Sand tiger pups look like adults,
but smaller.

Sand tiger pups are 37 to 41 inches (95 to 105 centimeters) long at birth. The pups are on their own when they are born. Sand tiger sharks live 15 to 16 years.

# Glossary

**dorsal fin**—a fin located on the back

**herd**—to gather animals in a group

**hunt**—to find and catch animals for food

**organ**—a body part that does a certain job

**prey**—an animal hunted by another animal for food

**pup**—a young shark

**snout**—the long front part of an animal's head; it includes the nose, mouth, and jaws

# Read More

**Ellwood, Nancy and Parrish, Margaret.** *Sharkpedia.* Second Edition. New York: DK Publishing, 2017.

**Hansen, Grace.** *Sand Tiger Sharks.* Sharks. Minneapolis: Abdo Kids, 2016.

**Meister, Cari.** *Sharks.* Life under the Sea. Minneapolis: Jump!, 2014.

# Internet Sites

FactHound offers a safe, fun way to find Internet sites related to this book. All of the sites on FactHound have been researched by our staff.

Here's all you do:

Visit *www.facthound.com*

Type in this code: 9781977101587

**Super-cool stuff!**

Check out projects, games and lots more at
**www.capstonekids.com**

## Critical Thinking Questions

1. Why do sand tiger sharks swallow air?

2. What body part helps sand tiger sharks find food?

3. How do sand tiger sharks work together to hunt?

## Index